My Look

a guide to fashion & style

Other books by Marlene Wallach

❉

My Beauty:
A Guide to Looking & Feeling Great

My Life:
A Guide to Health & Fitness

My Self:
A Guide to Me

marlene wallach
president, wilhelmina kids & teens modeling agency
WITH GRACE NORWICH

My Look

a guide to fashion & style

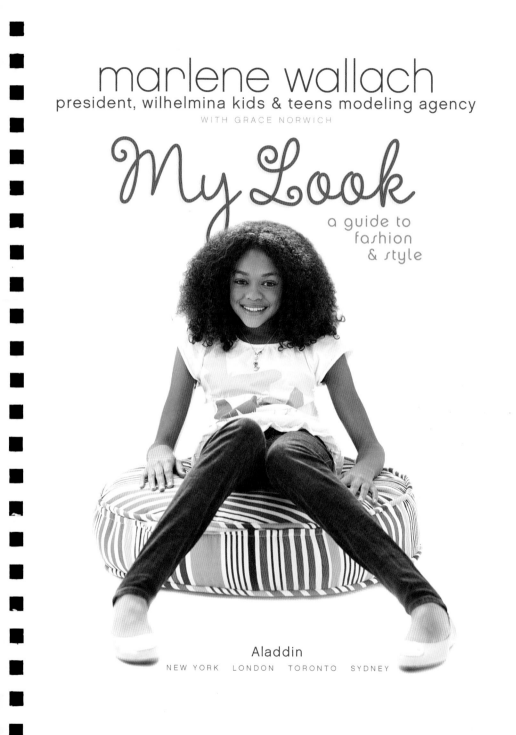

Aladdin
NEW YORK   LONDON   TORONTO   SYDNEY

ALADDIN

An imprint of Simon & Schuster Children's Publishing Division

1230 Avenue of the Americas, New York, NY 10020

Designed by Karin Paprocki

The text of this book was set in ITC Avant Garde Gothic.

Manufactured in China

First Aladdin edition August 2009

2 4 6 8 10 9 7 5 3 1

Library of Congress Cataloging-in-Publication Data

Wallach, Marlene. My look : a guide to fashion & style / by Marlene Wallach, with Grace Norwich.

p. cm. ISBN: 978-1-4169-7910-4 1. Girls' clothing—Juvenile literature. 2. Preteens—Clothing—

Juvenile literature. 3. Grooming for girls—Juvenile literature. I. Norwich, Grace. II. Title. TT562.

W35 2009 646.7′046—dc22 2008037370

To Stuart Wallach,
who had a unique style
of his very own

CONTENTS

My Look
a guide to fashion & style

a note
FROM MARLENE

HAVE YOU EVER WONDERED WHY models always look so amazing in fashion magazines and on the runway? Well, it's easy for them. They're surrounded by a team of professionals who create their look, from their carefully blown-out hair to their perfectly pedicured toes. There's one person to apply the makeup, one for hair, and there's even one to pick out the clothes! I'm here to tell that you can look just as amazing as a model without relying on an entourage of assistants, if you're willing to work on it.

You are special—with a style that's all your own. *My Look*

is all about helping your unique beauty shine through so that others can see how truly incredible you are. With essential tips and easy-to-follow guidelines, you'll find lots of tools to help you gain self-confidence and allow you to express yourself. In this book, I'm going to teach you the basic rules of fashion and share the secrets I've picked up from my years in the fashion and beauty businesses. You'll learn how to make your personal style dazzle so that you're as beautiful on the outside as you are inside.

Whether you know it or not, you already have your own sense of fashion and style. Your style has been in the works ever since you were too small to know what the word meant. You might have adored a certain pink sweater and wore it to shreds, but hated the yellow one that was a birthday present from your elderly aunt. That was the beginning of your sense of style. Or maybe you were the kid who showed up on picture day feeling awesome in a long-sleeved striped shirt under your sundress. Your unique style strikes again!

It's okay if some of your wardrobe choices when you were a little kid were major style don'ts; that's what we call experimentation. I'm going to take that passion for fashion and help you turn it into major style dos! Now is the best time for you to experiment with different looks. The great thing about it is that there are many fashion options to choose from. Of course, having more options means there are more ways to get into trouble. But relax. To ensure that you make a statement without sticking out like a sore thumb, I'll be here every step of the way.

chapter 1
DRESS THE PART

STYLE IS SOMETHING TO CELEBRATE. It's not just about plunking down a whole lot of cash at the mall to buy the latest trend worn by stars in celebrity magazines. It's true that debating what the look of the moment is with your best pals can be a lot of fun. But when people say, "That girl's got *style*," they're referring to something other than just her outfit. They're talking about how she looks in her clothes, how she carries herself, and the confidence she radiates.

Your best look is easy to find. The idea is to wear things that work for the unique person you are. That way, everyone will recognize the amazing person underneath that jacket or those jeans.

In other words, the place to start is recognizing that fashion has to fit your lifestyle. Are you a glam girl or an athletic type, or a little bit of both? If so, you'll have to make extra room in that closet! Do you live in the country, where heavy boots get you from the school bus to your front door during the winter? Or are you smack-dab in the middle of a big city, where comfortable shoes are a must for all the walking you do?

These factors will all enter into your personal sense of style. There's nothing less fashionable than forcing clothes into a situation where they really don't fit. For example, wearing your fanciest ballet skimmers on a muddy field to watch your best friend's soccer game wouldn't look cool. In fact, it would be just plain silly.

It's shocking, but true: There *is* a practical side to style.

It's all about your unique style—not just about fitting in.

Provided you follow some basic guidelines, it's good to shake things up. Mixing new items into your wardrobe is what it's about. Clothes can be a way to explore different sides of your personality. Let's say you're the class athlete. That doesn't mean you have to wear sweatshirts and sneakers night and day. Do the unexpected and wear a skirt—okay, it can be a jean skirt! You might be pleasantly surprised by the reactions you get and how free it makes you feel that you're not stuck in one look.

8

Discover where you fit on the FASHION spectrum. What follows is a questionnaire to get you thinking about your unique style. Fill it out to find out more about your likes and dislikes before we dive into the nitty-gritty of looking great.

I. **When you walk into your new room on the first day of school, you like to:**

A. have all eyes on you from the moment you open the door (1 point)

B. joke around with a few kids and introduce yourself to your new classmates (2 points)

C. blend into the background quietly until you have had a few days to check out the scene (3 points)

2. You wouldn't be caught dead in:

A. hand-me-downs (1 point)

B. jeans so tight they look painted on (2 points)

C. a red party dress (3 points)

3. You find yourself with extra allowance for raking the leaves and decide to spend the money on:

A. a new novel you've been dying to read (2 points)

B. a surprise frozen yogurt run for a few friends (3 points)

C. a tube of super-glossy lip gloss (1 point)

4. Your favorite time of day is:

A. the peace of morning before your hectic schedule begins (2 points)

B. right after school, hanging with your best buds (3 points)

C. at night, rocking out to your favorite tunes in your bedroom (1 point)

5. Your idea of the perfect date with your friends is:

A. a pizza, a rental movie, and a lot of freshly baked chocolate chip cookies (3 points)

B. a long day of biking with a jump into a pool at the end of the journey (2 points)

C. hanging out at the mall, scoping cute boys (1 point)

6. Your preferred mode of transportation to school is:

A. your own two feet (2 points)

B. whichever of your friends' parents have the nicest car (1 point)

C. the school bus, where you catch up on any missed gossip (3 points)

7. The first thing you reach for in the morning is:

A. your cell phone to check for missed text messages (3 points)

B. a mirror to check on that yucky pimple (1 point)

C. your diary to write down any dreams during the night (2 points)

8. When you're down, a real pick-me-up is:

A. talking to your mom over a big piece of cake (2 points)

B. helping out someone else, like a friend with homework or your sister with chores (3 points)

C. trying on your fanciest dress and shoes (1 point)

9. The idea of shopping for clothes makes you want to:

A. jump for joy (1 point)

B. run for the hills (2 points)

C. get a cute purse for your best friend (3points)

10. You're happiest when you are:

A. surrounded by your friends and family (3 points)

B. at the center of the dance floor (1 point)

C. taking a walk down your block listening to your favorite song (2 points)

If you had . . .

10–17 points:

YOU LOVE THE SPOTLIGHT AND IT LOVES YOU. STANDING out is what you do best. Shiny necklaces and dangly earrings are awesome accessories for you. And don't shy away from color. Even a pink T-shirt, paired with cute jeans, will come alive with your sparkling personality.

18–24 points:

YOU HAVE CLASSIC ELEGANCE AND POISE. QUIET AND thoughtful, you like to take life in measured steps. And how pretty those steps are! Bold, clean, solid colors, like navy and white, go wonderfully with your style. Little pearl earrings and ballet flats make your heart sing. Your look will take you far.

25–30 points:

EVERYONE'S BEST FRIEND, YOU'RE SWEET AND CARING. Comfortable clothes are an absolute must for you. But that doesn't mean you have to sacrifice style. A sleek fleece, boot-cut jeans, and cool sneakers are not only cute but will get you on your way. And with all your extracurricular activities, you don't have that much time to devote to clothes. That's why each piece in your wardrobe has to be a winner—just like you!

chapter 2

BE YOUR OWN
BEST DESIGNER

THERE WOULDN'T BE A SINGLE SHIRT, skirt, or pair of pants if it weren't for clothing designers. Fashion begins with these super-talented professionals, referred to as *creatives*—the people who create and design in the fashion world.

Each designer follows elements of the same basic process, regardless of how big a name they may have in the industry. First, from their rich imagination they sketch ideas for the new garments to be made for the season. Next they select fabrics for their creations. Finally they have the outfits

sewn together to create samples from which the garments are mass-produced. Some of the finished pieces are hits. Some are misses. It's important to remember that before even the first stitch is sewn for a line of clothing, a designer has to use his or her fundamental understanding of cut and color so the clothes on the fashion runway and in school hallways will look equally great. It's important that you spend the time to read and understand the following design basics. They will be your tools when you begin to work with your wardrobe.

Let's break it down.

Coco Chanel

(1883–1971) was a famous French designer. She revolutionized designer clothing of the time with the introduction of comfortable, casual dresses and suits when the market was dominated by clothing with constricting corsets. Her designer label—and iconic designs—can still be seen all over the world today.

COLOR CODE

NOTHING AFFECTS MOOD QUITE like color. That's why poets write about the pink blush of a rose or the golden rays of a sunset. Colors bring up feelings in us that can change our day and can even bring back a memory—like that beautiful sunset or that deep blue sea. Color is also the best way to highlight something—think about that bright red ink on white paper whenever a teacher is grading! It's no wonder color is one of the most important tools designers have to work with in creating clothing. Sometimes a designer decides to plan a whole fashion line around a single color, or even a single shade of a color. What does this have to do with you? Well, you have your favorite colors and those you don't care for much. But do you ever think about what colors you wear and why? You should, since color is as crucial to the success of your style as to whether or not your pants fit.

Come on, and let's dive into the vibrant world of color.

What Colors Should You Wear?

SEE WHAT COLORS SUIT YOU BEST. WE'RE

talking about the colors that go best with your hair,

eye, and skin tones.

Blondes with blue or green eyes: Earth

tones such as browns, golds, yellows, and

greens are a natural way to go with this

coloring.

hot chocolate

gold rush

emerald isle

Brunettes or blondes with pinkish

skin tone: Pastels—whether pink, blue, or

yellow—make this skin glow. Pastels in floral

patterns are equally lovely. Patterns are nice

to consider for this group.

ballet pink

sunshine

spring

tangerine

fern

latte

Brunettes or redheads with freckles:

Orange—a color that not everyone can wear—

looks awesome on these girls. Dark

19

yellow, green, and beige make excellent accent colors.

Dark brown hwith olive skin: This group shines in colors that have a splash of shimmering gold, brown, or dark purple.

Dark brown or black hair with dark skin: Go for bold colors—but don't go overboard. Shades of gold, purple, pink, and blue look great with darker complexions.

Color Tip

HERE'S A TRICK TO PRACTICE WITH COLOR and figure out your favorites: Head to your neighborhood paint store and check out the paint chips they have in stock. See which colors you're attracted to and ask for samples that you can take home. Go with a parent, so you don't feel too shy about asking. When you get home, take a look in the mirror and hold the chips up to your face. How do they look?

If the color makes your complexion look livelier, you've got a winner. If the color makes your face look washed out, throw that chip away.

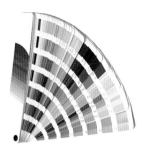

Go through all the chips and compare the flattering colors with the clothes in your closet. Do you have any clothes in those colors? What do you own that complements them? Next time you go shopping, bring a few of the chips as a reminder of what colors work for you.

Check the Temperature

WHEN YOU SELECT A COLOR TO WEAR, YOU should consider how light or dark it is. Generally speaking, people tend to wear darker colors in the winter and lighter shades in the summer. There is a practical reason for this, since lighter shades keep you cooler in hotter months. But the shade of a color isn't all about practicality. A pale pink may come off as demure, while a deep, hot pink says, "Watch out!"

The two extremes of the color spectrum are black and white—two colors that fashion has had a field day experimenting with. Let's deal with white first. You might have heard the saying, "Don't wear white after Labor Day." Well, that isn't just some stuffy rule of fashion etiquette. It's based on the idea you already know now: White is a good choice when it's warm outside. White is awesome for summer— it works well with pastels and looks great with sun-kissed skin— but these days the rule about white during winter is flexible. Winter white is a great pick-me-up on a dreary January day, and it complements darker skin tones. As a matter of fact, darker skin tones look great in light colors no matter what time of year it is, so go for it!

When it comes to black, less is more. It's best to use sparingly, because the darkest color in the palette can end up making you look like you're on your way to a funeral. Consider replacing black with rich, earthy colors, those colors and shades found in nature. They complement all skin tones and are perfect to wear in the colder months. Many different shades of brown and green are found in the most fashionable clothes, season after season. Another great option is navy blue, one of the chicest colors around. Versatile navy is terrific in the winter, paired with

neutrals, or in the summer with a white T-shirt for a nautical look that never goes out of style. Another bonus of navy: It does a great job hiding stains.

A Bright Attitude

WHEN YOU PUT ON A KELLY GREEN SWEATER or fire-engine red raincoat, don't be surprised if people take notice of you. Bright colors attract attention, so it takes confidence to wear them. Hold people's gaze as they check you out and smile back. And remember, it's okay if you don't feel so bold every day. It's perfectly fine to put on easy-to-wear warm browns and earth tones when you don't want all that attention being drawn to yourself.

Bright colors can be also the perfect shot in the arm. Instead of putting on that big, baggy sweater when you're feeling down in the dumps, see how your mood changes when

White

keeps you cool in hot weather because it doesn't absorb sunlight, and it should be a regular in your summer wardrobe. Black does absorb sunlight, so it's no wonder there are so many black winter coats!

you put on your hot pink top or your favorite sparkly necklace. Bold colors can lift sagging spirits, and fast!

Don't Overdo It

COLOR IS LIKE EATING CHOCOLATE OR
talking on the phone: You *can* have too much of a good
thing. Remember the saying, "Less is more." That's certainly
true when it comes to color.

What's true for bright colors is also true for patterns. While
there are beautifully designed dresses with stripes and polka
dots, you might want to save those patterns for a great
accent piece to perk up an outfit, or for special occasions.
Who doesn't love herringbone tights with a solid skirt and an
outfit with different textures? But don't wear a pattern head
to toe, or wear different patterns in one outfit, unless you are
really experienced in mixing patterns and know you have it
just right.

SIZE YOURSELF UP: THE IMPORTANCE OF A GOOD FIT

NO MATTER HOW CUTE THAT DRESS in the store is, if it doesn't fit, back on the rack it goes. You don't see models on the runway with clothes that don't fit. If clothes are too tight, you can look like you're wearing something that was in the dryer for too long. And for those of you hiding in that sweatshirt down to your knees, come out, come out, wherever you are! Clothes that are too baggy not only make you look like you're wearing a potato sack, they usually make you look heavier than you really are. Yes, it's true! Like Goldilocks said at the three bears' house, it has to be "just right." What does that mean when it comes to clothes?

waist fit

- Skirts and pants should sit at the waist or slightly below, on the hips.

• For pants, the crotch should not ride up and make a V between your legs—when that happens, it could be that the cut doesn't work for you, or you need to try the next size. The pants are too big if the crotch hangs down more than half an inch. The fit should be comfortable but not too baggy.

• When it comes to shirts and jackets, shoulder seams should meet at the shoulder's edge, not go beyond. Here's an easy test to check for the proper fit of a jacket or a shirt: If you can't easily lift your arms or if the buttons pull, try a bigger size.

shoulder's edge

Memo from Marlene

Rolling up your sleeves on a favorite shirt can completely change the way it looks. Try it, and you'll have two shirts for the price of one.

27

Number Play

FOR KIDS' CLOTHING, THE IDEA IS THAT SIZES match up with age. So if you are twelve years old, you are supposed to wear a size twelve. *Supposed to.* Just take a look at your friends—do they all match up in height and weight? No way. It's just a guideline.

Whatever the size, don't get hung up on it. What may be a size 12 from one store or designer could fit totally differently in another. That's why when you go shopping you should always try on clothes that you want to buy. Even if it's a drag and you're in a rush, take the time to do so. And remember, the number on the clothing tag doesn't mean you're big or small or have anything to do with you at all. It's just a number.

One Size Doesn't ALWAYS Fit All

PEOPLE ARE LIKE SNOWFLAKES—EACH ONE of you is your own unique self. You may have a long torso, or supershort legs, which can make it difficult to find clothes that fit. If you find yourself with a common problem in many different stores and styles—like a gap in the waist of your pants—there is help. Sometimes your mom or a tailor can fix the one thing that's wrong with a garment that otherwise fits. It might be fun to try tying a sash through two belt loops to adjust the waistband, or using other accessories to fix a small problem as an alternative to alterations. If all else fails, a well-placed safety pin can usually do the trick, but be careful!

Memo from Marlene

Okay, if you're really, really, really obsessed with a dress that's a little too snug, try every single one that the store has in your size. Machines at the factory don't always cut the fabric exactly the same, so you might find one that's just a little bigger. Hey, that's a tip from *my* mom—and she's right. It sometimes works.

29

FASHION FINDS

Fashion can be daunting. There are so many elements that go into style, and inspiration for clothing is everywhere around you. Designers can get an idea for a dress by looking at a sculpture in a museum or find the perfect pair of shoes for a gown in a flea market. Fashion can be an all-consuming profession, with inspiration and fun ideas around every corner. That's why those who work in it find handy-dandy ways to keep track of all their projects and passions. And now you can use the same tools in planning your outfits. With these tricks of the trade, you're on your way to being a pro.

My Notes

Always be sure to test zippers and buttons, and check the stitching and belt loops (if any), before you head for the cashier.

Create Your Own
Style-Inspired Mood Wall

MOST DESIGNERS HAVE A WALL IN THEIR
studio covered with photos of male and female models,
scenes of beach sunsets, fabric swatches of exotic patterns,
classical art images, and other things that inspire. This is known
as their Mood Wall. Whenever the mood strikes with an image,
a pattern, or a look, it becomes a part of this always-changing
collage.

In the same spirit, here's a page of fashion finds and space
for you to add some of your own finds. Cut and paste exciting

styles from magazines and catalogs,
and snapshots of things you really like.
If a mannequin in the window or a
dress hanging on the rack catches
your eye, take a photo. You can also
sketch ideas from your imagination
and include them, too. There are no
limits as to what you might find, or to
your style—experiment!

31

Create your own
Mood Wall

CREATING YOUR LOOK
THE LOOK BOOK WAY

A DESIGNER CREATES A NEW LINE OF clothes to sell to stores for the upcoming season and in order to promote the fabulous new fashions in that collection, a Look Book is created and distributed to people connected to the business. In the Look Book all the new pieces in the line are featured for magazine editors to write about and for store buyers to purchase. It's an organized and exciting way to see all the latest looks in one place.

Here's your chance to create your own Look Book using five basic pieces. See how many great outfits you can get from these simple fashion staples:

1. Pair of dark jeans

2. White button-down shirt

3. Skirt (not too short)

4. Cardigan sweater

5. Colored shirt

Preppy: Turn yourself into instant Ivy League material by rolling up the sleeves of the white button-down to your elbows and turning up the collar. A short strand of pearls or another necklace that hits your collarbone adds a nice touch of class to the look. Now you're ready for the country-club scene!

Sporty

Sporty: Comfort and mobility are key to this outfit. Wear the colored shirt with your favorite shorts—not the workout variety, but crisp cotton or denim. Tie the cardigan sweater around your waist for an on-the-go feel or throw it over your shoulders for warmth if you need it.

Preppy

Rock 'n' Roll

Rock 'n' Roll: Get in touch with your inner wild child by throwing on the dark jeans and white button-down. Layer the shirt over it for an unexpected indie twist. Finish with a pair of high-tops, and you're rockin'.

Glam Girl: The skirt is a must. Instead of wearing it with the white button-down shirt, which would be too stark for the fun side of you, pair it with a colored shirt. Tuck in your shirt for a more prim look. Accessorize with a matching headband and delicate earrings for lunch with your gal pals.

Glam Girl

Mix 'n' Match

ONCE YOU HAVE SPENT SOME TIME EXPERI-
menting with the basics of fashion, it's time to take your experience to the next level. Why do some outfits look great, even though you just threw them together without a care, but some don't make the grade no matter how long you stare in the mirror? It might seem like luck, but there are actually basic principles and elements of design at work. With these concepts under your belt, you'll understand the underlying reasons your favorite shirt looks so cute with a pair of shorts.

Here's a game to test your knowledge of design principles and help you learn how to use them in real life. See if you can match the photos to their correct captions, then practice these concepts.

Texture: This is how an article of clothing feels to the touch or how you think it would feel when looking at it. The texture of an item can go from scratchy to silky soft.

Do It Yourself: Go through your closet and touch all your clothes. What textures do you love? Which ones are turnoffs? Ask yourself if you tend to wear the clothes with the textures you like more and avoid textures you dislike. Try pairing opposites—such as a wool sweater and linen skirt—for some fun and fresh combinations.

Emphasis: This is an element in the design that immediately catches your eye and stands out from the rest of the dress, shirt, or pants—it's the focus. The focus can be a change in the pattern, a logo, or add-ons such as buttons, sequins, or ribbon.

Do It Yourself: Take a pair of old jeans that have been pushed to the back of the closet and give them new life by heading out to a trimming store and picking up ornate patches, beads, and ribbons. See what catches your eye and what will work with the jeans. Sew patches onto back pockets or add a ribbon trim to the cuffs. The new emphasis may change the way you see your old jeans.

Proportion: This is the relationship between different design elements in one article of clothing and how different parts of an outfit relate to one another. The squares in a pattern on a shirt shouldn't be so big that they look boxy, or so small that they disappear. Proportion is at work when oversize pants are kept in check with a fitted shirt.

Do It Yourself:
Gather a large shirt—maybe a big sweatshirt or your older sister's button-down—a slim-fitting T-shirt, a flowing skirt, and your skinniest jeans. You can lay them all out on your bed to get an overview. Try on all the different combinations

40

you can make with these four items. Throw in a belt or sash to really shake it up. Ask yourself which ones work and which don't. How do the laws of proportion apply?

Rhythm: This is the repetition of lines, color, or shapes in a pattern. The use of rhythm—say, baby blue polka dots on a dress that are picked up in a similar baby blue trim—draws your eye from one part of the design to another.

Do It Yourself: Head out to a crafts store and pick six different kinds of beads, and elastic to string them on. They can be any type or color of bead—plastic, metal, green, orange, patterned, and so on. The idea is to create different bracelet designs by stringing the beads in unique patterns. For example, a simple variety for one bracelet could be a pattern of two different types of beads repeated over and over. Or you could use just one kind of bead. Let your creative juices flow. Experiment and have some fun with it—use all the beads at once and see what that pattern looks like. Once you are done, stack three or four bracelets on your wrist. Check out how they look. See how the different colors and patterns look mixed together.

Unity: This is when all the elements of your outfit work together harmoniously. Unity can be achieved in many different ways—through similar colors, shapes, or styles. Dressed entirely in different shades of cream, or all in pieces with straight lines in the pattern, or, let's say, in sixties hippie items, you'll certainly be put together.

Do It Yourself: Take one of your favorite outfits and look at the individual style elements. Figure out the unifying elements of the outfit. Is it tailored? Or does each piece have a small fabric pattern? Once you have identified the common theme, choose an accessory that is also unifying in its style. Maybe your headband is the same or a similar color, maybe your shoes. Experiment, and you'll be able to pull together an amazing outfit.

If you overdo it, you'd better know what you're doing.

chapter 3
HIGH STYLIN'

Fashion, like everything else, is all about the details. Would dangly earrings dress up an outfit or make you look like a Christmas tree? Does that black shirt look too dreary on a rainy day? These little things can make a big difference in your final look. On a photo shoot, the stylist is in charge of all these things. Yes, there are professionals whose sole job it is to outfit the models with their wardrobe—clothing and accessories. They put it all together for the model to wear on a shoot or on the runway. Here's everything you need to know from the pros to style yourself and to create a fabulous outfit.

Don't Be Too Matchy-Matchy

MIXING AND MATCHING IS A REAL ART, AND one you can master with practice. Here's the deal: Whether the clothes are high fashion or from the local Army-Navy store, a good stylist never puts an entire outfit together from one company or one designer. Taking a T-shirt from one place and mixing it with a skirt from another and a jacket from a third store will instantly give your look a unique style.

Also, try to mix up styles of clothes. Don't wear a sporty or flirty look head to toe. Pair a boyish white tank top with a flowery skirt, or jeans with a fancy top. Try different textures. The contrast will get you noticed.

It's Okay to Wear Your Favorites a Lot

FRENCH WOMEN ARE OFTEN THOUGHT TO be the most chic (pronounced *sheek*) in the world, and here's how they do it: They wear their favorites a lot. They buy a

couple of things they love, and they wear them over and over and over. This practice is partly a result of the high cost of buying clothes; they would rather have a couple of very special things than lots of "throwaways." They may have a favorite sweater that they really like and wear so often that it becomes their signature piece. It's a reflection of something unique about them.

If there's a certain sweater or a pair of pants that makes *you* feel great and you want to reach for it almost every day, then do it! Just keep it clean and change the other elements of your look. If someone teases you about wearing the same thing regularly, tell them *you've* decided on a repeat performance. If they don't know that's the way the truly stylish do it, just let them know it's your signature piece. *Ooh la la!*

SHOP TILL YOU DROP

In Your Own Closet

DON'T FORGET TO CHECK OUT WHAT GOT pushed to the back of your closet or what's at the bottom of the drawer. It's amazing what you can find when shopping in your own closet. Take stock of all the cool stuff you already have in your wardrobe, and be sure to make a pile of the clothes that don't fit or that you never wear (for more on closet organizing, see page 90). Consider donating that pile to a charity—it will make you feel good and free up room for—what else?—more clothes!

Trading with Friends

SOME OF THE CLOTHES IN YOUR GIVEAWAY pile may no longer be right for you, but would be a great look on one of your friends. Set aside those items for a swap session. Get your gal pals together for an afternoon where everyone brings things they don't wear anymore (check your "trade picks" with your parents first). Something your best friend never wears might become your go-to getup. You might have loved that hat in the boutique but at home realize it just doesn't go with anything you have. We all make "mis-buys" once in a while; the thing is to do something about it. After all, one girl's trash is another girl's treasure.

Shop at Mom's

RAIDING YOUR MOM'S OR SISTER'S CLOSET— with permission, of course—is the perfect way to sass up your look. There might be an old sweater she hasn't worn in ages that's back in fashion and that you can wear as a dress. You and your mom most likely don't share the same sense of style, but she may have a scarf that would look cool as a belt or other items that you can transform. Remember that as a rule, mother knows best. If she says something doesn't look quite right, just take her word for it. She's had a lot more experience with this than you have. Ask to see pictures of her in some outfits she thinks are crazy now and laugh about it together. Who knows? You just might be inspired!

Sales, Sales, Sales!

YOU DON'T NEED A HUGE BANK ACCOUNT or a credit card in order to look amazing. The thing is, you should save your fun shopping (we're not talking about back-to-school necessities and socks) for sale time. On the day after Thanksgiving—the biggest shopping day of the year—and on just about every other major holiday, stores slash their prices. That's the time to beg Mom for that fabulous top you can't live without. Be sure to ask the store about its return policy, and don't take the price tag off until you're absolutely sure you love it.

My Notes
A sale is only a sale if you buy something you'll wear. If the garment is a dress, close your eyes and picture the dress in your closet. Is it THE dress you'd pick to wear? If the answer is no, back it goes.

Fashion Recycling

FOLLOW THE MODELS AND OTHER FASHION types and go vintage. You may have turned your nose up at your local consignment shop or Salvation Army store, but you could be missing out on treasures galore. The major benefit to finding a cool top or funky belt at a thrift shop is that you'll *never* see anyone else in school wearing the same one. And don't forget, thrift stores can be really inexpensive. That's why they're called "thrift" stores, after all! There's a great sense of pride in finding something really cool that's really affordable. And there's another benefit— the money you spend at those stores goes to good causes. So you can shop and feel good about yourself.

Reality Check

This is simple. If it doesn't fit, or the fabric makes you itchy, back on the rack it goes. It may be the most beautiful dress in the world, and it may break your heart not to buy it, but if it's not really right, it'll end up in a mounting giveaway pile in your closet. Don't worry, there will be other "perfect" dresses.

Make a Wish List

A CHANGE OF SEASON IS THE PERFECT TIME

to create a wish list of things you need and want for your wardrobe. Fill out the list below so that you're prepared when you head to the store.

I want:	I need:

Ask a Stylist

What's something every girl should have in her wardrobe?

A REALLY GREAT PAIR OF SHOES. NO MATTER WHAT YOU have on, shoes can change the look. Try a pair with a little sparkle, shine, or print. Something different. Shoes that are lighthearted and show your personality. Even if you're more tentative about branching out in your wardrobe, you feel freer to do it with your shoes.

Memo from Marlene

I used to see my older sister, Maxine, stuff her shoes with newspaper when they were soaked from the rain. I do the same thing now, since it helps them keep their shape while they dry. Sometimes it's worth it to listen to your older sister!

What's your best piece of fashion advice?

FASHION IS JUST FOR FUN. Don't take it too seriously. Always be as free as you were when you were four years old. Your clothes will look a lot better that way.

—CHRIS O'SHEA, STYLIST

ACCESSORIES, ACCESSORIES, ACCESSORIES

BAGS, BELTS, JEWELRY, AND ANYTHING else that adorns your outfit can make or break a look. Here's how to be on the right side of that equation.

Scarves

HAVE YOU EVER THOUGHT ABOUT THE FACT that scarves have two different functions? They are (a) for warmth and (b) a style accessory. They can add color and texture to an outfit and can be worn in many different ways. The three styles shown illustrate different ways to wear your muffler without your winter coat, any time of the year. You've probably seen kids at school take off their coats and wear their scarves with just a shirt or a sweater in colder weather. It's kind of a cool, bohemian look and gives your scarf extra fashion mileage.

Glamorous: For an instantly sophisticated look, take a square silky scarf and fold it on the diagonal. Knot the two ends in the front near your collarbone, and voilà, you could be coming from the offices of a fashion magazine.

Drama: A superlong, thin scarf that hangs around your neck with no knot is a surefire way to add drama to any outfit.

Double Drama: Wrap a silky scarf around your head and knot it in the back to create a headband, and soon people will be asking, "Who's the movie star?"

Belts

IF YOU THINK THESE ARE FOR KEEPING YOUR pants up, you've got it all wrong. Belts can be as exciting and beautiful as a piece of jewelry when worn in the right way. And don't just look at belts as belts. One of your father's old ties can work well as a belt—or a tie!

WIDTH MATTERS

The most fashionable belts by far are often at extremes—superwide or super-skinny. Wide ones look great cinched around your middle for a more soph-isticated look. Skinny belts are nice accents for delicate dresses.

WHERE TO WEAR?

At the waist, a belt gives your clothes definition. Wear one with a slight tilt for a more relaxed look. A belt also acts as a unifier for

Memo from Marlene

When wearing a belt over your clothes, don't forget to "blouse" your shirt or sweater to ease the look—a loose fit that extends to the waist or slightly below and hangs over the belt. *TRÈS* CHIC!

different elements of an outfit: jeans and tops, a blouse and a skirt. Play with it a little and you'll get it right. Around the hips, a belt will define a dress or sweater in a more casual way.

Bag Sense

CALL IT A BAG, HANDBAG, PURSE, BACK-pack, or pocketbook, there are almost as many of them in the stores as there are stars in the sky. Remember, there are some important tips to keep in mind when you go on your bag-buying spree.

COMFORT

If it's really heavy without anything inside, drop it and don't look back! If it's weighing you down without a single notebook, hairbrush, or cell phone, that bag will become a real back-breaker the first day out. Not for you.

SECURITY

Because you keep your valuables in your handbag, you want it to close securely to keep out wandering hands. A zipper or a clasp will usually do the trick, but give it a test and see if you can sneak your hand in an unsecured opening. If that's the case, it's not for you. That's the surest way to lose your cell phone.

EAƧE

Choose a bag with a long strap that goes over your shoulder and crosses your chest easily for parties and dances. This is the best for dancing with your pals in comfort and style! A bag with a long strap also works for everyday. Choose one in a neutral color like brown, or a casual, fun fabric.

Jewelry

THERE IS AN IMPORTANT PRINCIPLE KNOWN as KISS, which stands for Keep It Simple, Stupid. This principle is totally appropriate for wearing jewelry. When it comes time to make a choice, choose from dangly earrings, a necklace, or bracelets, but not all at once, or you'll look like a jewelry display. Coco Chanel, the legendary designer mentioned earlier, put it best when she said to look in the mirror and

always take one thing off before you leave the house. Your accessory for an outfit can be as simple as wearing a ribbon in place of your watchband. Resist the temptation to go overboard!

Eyeglasses

MOVIE STARS HAVE BEEN KNOWN TO WEAR fake eyeglasses just to look cool. Nowadays there are all kinds of fun and glamorous frames, so you can find ones that match your style perfectly. To make it easier to choose, bring a parent and a good friend when you go shopping for glasses. Your decision will rest partially on their opinion, since you can't see without your glasses! Even if you're buying sunglasses and can see perfectly, it helps to get a second opinion.

Memo from Marlene

Remember, for glasses to stay comfortable, get them tightened every month.

WARDROBE DIARY

FASHION PROFESSIONALS KEEP WARD-robe diaries of what they wear to interview for jobs. Those interviews are called castings. The wardrobe diary is to keep track of outfits that make them feel like they can book the job. Now you can do it too. When you assemble a killer ensemble, fill out an entry in your very own wardrobe diary to remember how it felt. You can even have someone take a photo of you and paste it on the page. Describe your experience of wearing the outfit: Did it change your look? Did people treat you differently? What else did you like about it? Would you change anything next time around?

Check out a few entries from thirteen-year-old Aliyah's real-life wardrobe diary.

Event: Regular school day

Outfit description: It started off with the shoes: white sneakers with a green alligator.

Top: Searching through the closet is always a task, but I was lucky to find the perfect green T-shirt to match.

Bottom: To mix it up, I chose plaid shorts with silver stripes.

Shoes: See above.

Accessories: I chose silver accessories—tiny silver hoops, a silver belt, and my silver book bag.

Thoughts: I call this look "comfortable with a twist."

Event: Shopping with friends

Outfit description: My top was the focus of this outfit.

Top: It was a white tunic with yellow and peach butterflies—it's loose and soft.

Bottom: Dark denim skinny jeans.

Shoes: Yellow flats that go well with the yellow butterfly.

Accessories: Gold stud earrings.

Thoughts: I wanted to look like a pop star. It's not always easy finding something to wear, and I'm always going back and forth. When I can't choose, I ask my mom.

My Wardrobe Diary

Event:

Your photo here!

Outfit description:

Top:

Bottom:

Shoes:

Accessories:

Thoughts:

My Wardrobe Diary

Event:

Your photo here!

Outfit description:

Top:

Bottom:

Shoes:

Accessories:

Thoughts:

FASHION SHOWS ARE ONE OF THE most exciting parts of the fashion industry. Designers prepare for months and spend millions of dollars for about fifteen minutes of models strutting down the runway. Yes, that's really how long a professional fashion show lasts. The shows are short but super-glamorous, with stars in the front rows sizing up the latest, coolest clothes. Well, who says celebrities should have all the fun? Here's the A to Z on how to produce a fashion show in your very own living room. It might not land you a design contract, but you'll have a fun time with friends.

Pick a Team

AFTER YOU GET PERMISSION FROM YOUR parents to put on a fashion show at home, your first assignment is to pick a team. To make your show a smashing success, you'll need a lot of folks to help out. First off, there are the models—what's a fashion show without models? Ask friends with a variety of different looks if they want to be in this amazing fashion show you're producing. In addition, you'll need a few more friends to work behind the scenes, helping you run the show. This team is referred to as your *production staff*. The production staff includes a *coordinator* to keep the show on track and a *wardrobe mistress* to make sure the outfits are clean, pressed, and ready to go. Then there's the *stylist*. The stylist puts together the outfits, just like the way you put the different pieces together on your bed. The thing is, the stylist has to do it for all the outfits, and also has to coordinate all the accessories with the outfits. It's a big job, so select someone who really wants to do it. You can also split the job between two people and give each person half the outfits to be responsible for. And of course you will want to have photos of this amazing event, so a photographer is a must. Pick a friend or family member who will tell jokes or make funny faces to lighten the mood and keep the models smiling. This is *your* show, and you call the shots. And don't forget, you'll need an audience, too. Invite friends with a fun e-mail or a phone call.

74

Pick a Theme

LET YOUR MIND RUN WILD. THE THEME could be based on a color, like red, or a style, like eighties punk, or an occasion, like back to school. It can be just about anything, so have fun. Take an inventory of what clothes you and your friends have in their closets. This will help you come up with your theme.

Pick the Outfits

GO THROUGH YOUR CLOSET AND THE CLOSETS of your friends and production staff to come up with five to ten ensembles that match your theme. Remember to consider your models when crafting the outfits—will they feel comfortable in your designs? You want them to feel good, not foolish. Lay each outfit on the bed or the floor (if it's clean!) to see how they look as a group, and also decide the best order for the outfits. A knockout to start off with can get everyone's attention. And you—the last one on the catwalk—

should have a killer outfit. When it comes to accessories, think outside the box. A scarf can act as a belt. A belt can become a super-funky necklace. High fashion is all about experimentation!

Pick the Music

YOUR TUNES CAN TURN A GOOD FASHION show into a *great* fashion show. When you and your friends are strutting down the catwalk, you'll want to be really pumped, and there's no better way to do that than by cranking your favorite songs. Pick a few songs and compose your playlist. Once you have it set, practice walking to the music to see if the songs are too fast or too slow for the mood.

Pick Out a Cute Outfit for *You*

WHETHER YOU MAKE YOURSELF THE PRO-ducer or a model, you should be the last one down the runway. And it should be one grand entrance, so make sure you look great. Hey, it's only professional: The designer sets the standard for the show.

Pick Out Snacks

CREATE A CRAFT SERVICE TABLE—THAT'S
the professional term for "snack area."
Be sure to include healthy snacks like
carrots sticks, nuts, and raisins (see
My Life and JustAskMarlene.com for
more healthy snacks).

Pick the Lineup

THE LINEUP AND THE TIMING ARE VERY
important to the show. Also, be sure to give yourself enough
time to style your models in between walks. Don't be a diva
if a friend doesn't feel comfortable in one of your "designs."
Offer alternatives or change the outfit entirely. Remember,
feeling good is the key to looking good. If your model is
happy, she'll shine on the catwalk. Plus, creative solutions
are the mark of a great designer. Before the models have
been styled, pick out the order they should walk down the
runway and write it down for your coordinator. Once the
show starts, keep everyone moving! A "You look divine,

*daaa*rling!" is a great send-off for your models before they make their entrance and walk the walk.

Time for the Runway

CREATING A RUNWAY CAN BE AS SIMPLE AS moving some furniture around. If you are having the fashion show in your living room, after rearranging the furniture, you can just take crepe-paper streamers to create borders on each side of the walking path for the models. You don't actually have to "build" a runway to create the feel of a special passageway. And don't forget, after all your models have walked the runway, it's your turn! Swish and sashay on down with attitude. And when you've completed your walk, take a deep and graceful bow and let the clapping continue. Stand up straight, nod your head and smile, then gracefully turn around and walk off the runway, smiling from one side to the other as you go. CONGRATULATIONS on a huge success!

Go Pro

IF YOU LOVED THE EXPERIENCE OF YOUR
very own fashion show, you might want to consider going
to the next level: hosting one in your local school or library.
You can even charge admission and donate the money to
your favorite charity. This will be like the one in your living room
times a million. But before you go big-time, sit down and talk
over your plans with your parents—it's a big deal and a lot
of work.

Memo from Marlene

One thing a lot of people may
not realize is that a professional
fashion show typically lasts no more
than twenty minutes! Don't worry
about yours being too short—it'll
be the perfect amount to get
all your friends down the
runway.

chapter 4

LOOKING GREAT,
FEELING GREAT

NOW YOU'RE READY TO TAKE YOUR fashion savvy to the next level. That means learning about which clothes are best for your body type and the essentials for looking and feeling like a million bucks. Once you've found the shirts, dresses, pants, and sweaters that make up your style, your outfits are ready to jump into real life, so let's go!

ANATOMY LESSON

WHAT'S AN ANATOMY LESSON doing in a book about fashion and style? Fashion has as much to do with your size, your shape, and the way you carry yourself as it does with the clothes you wear. This isn't always the easiest subject to talk about, but the fact is your body is changing, and things may be happening that you're not totally comfortable with. Everybody—even a model—has some part of their body that they don't like. But fashion and style can sometimes be just the thing to turn those feelings around so that you feel great about yourself. As part of your wardrobe diary, you should write "I am beautiful" ten times a day for the next year. You will begin to see the power of these words.

How Your Body Relates to Your Clothes and Accessories

ARE YOU THE TALLEST GIRL IN THE CLASS?

You're lucky to be able to pull off wearing oversize bags and chunkier jewelry that won't get lost on your long, beautiful shape. If you're self-conscious about your size, you may gravitate to little pearl earrings or a tiny purse, but that will just make you look like you've stolen items out of a munchkin's closet.

ARE YOU PETITE?

Look for delicate necklaces and earrings. Avoid prints with large shapes. They can overwhelm your small frame.

How Your Body Parts Relate to One Another

EVERYONE'S BODY IS DIFFERENT, AND here are four areas that girls typically worry about, with tricks for clothes that flatter.

SKINNY LEGS

Wear skirts or pants that add to your lower half, such as:

- Flare and A-line skirts, and skirts with pleats
- Wide-legged jeans

skinny legs

bigger on bottom

- Light-colored pants and skirts
- Pants with patterns; slightly flared pants

BIGGER ON THE BOTTOM

Make the most out of those curves with:

- Straight-leg or boot-leg pants
- Darker bottoms, low-cut pants, and flared skirts

NARROW ON THE TOP

Add volume to your top with:

- Light-colored tops; blouses with design work, ruffles, and scoop necks
- Shirts with horizontal stripes
- Dresses that cinch at the waist

narrow on the top

broad shoulders

BROAD SHOULDERS

Wear shirts that minimize your top:

- Darker tops and V-necks
- Medium-size necklaces

Think Tall

IF YOU HOLD YOURSELF WITH CONFIDENCE

and walk tall, people will think you *are* confident. Whether you're long and lean or curvy, body shape is only a part of your overall look. Another big part is how you carry yourself. Confidence is beautiful in any shape.

STAND UP STRAIGHT

Lots of famous fashion models talk about how they hated being the tallest kid in the class and how they slouched and curled their shoulders in. Yes, even models were teased by their classmates! But slouching doesn't just make you appear shorter, it makes you look sloppy. Whether you're four feet or six feet tall, stand straight with your shoulders back for a stance that's not only good-looking, but also good for you. For more tips on good posture, see *My Life*.

SMILE

No matter what you're wearing and no matter how gorgeous you are, your smile is your best accessory. Wear it. Use it. Flaunt it. There's a famous model who says she has about 250 different smiles that she practices in the mirror. Look in the mirror and see if you can come up with three different smiles to start—and no fake smiles, please.

MYTHS ABOUT BODY TYPE

• Bigger girls should hide their size under big clothes. No way. Not true. Forget it. Well-fitting pants, structured blouses, and jackets are fabulous on anyone. A pair of great-fitting pants is always a good solution. Trying to mask your shape under big sweatshirts, sweatpants, tees, and jeans only winds up looking sloppy. You should always accent what you have with clothes that flatter you. Flaunt it, don't hide it!

Memo from Marlene

When you're nervous, your smile can look forced. To help make it look more natural, place your tongue behind your two front teeth on the inside. This relaxes your facial muscles, and your smile will look camera pretty.

• Petite girls can't wear wide-legged pants or flowing skirts. They can, but it's all about proportion. Make sure you keep your top small so your entire outfit isn't oversize. A fitted tee or cropped sweater will do the trick.

• Only girls with super-skinny legs can wear short skirts. Actually, micro-minis are only cool for models on the runway. They don't have to worry about the impracticality of a skirt this length. A good choice for your skirt length is always an A-line or straight skirt that falls a few inches above the knee for a hip and flattering look on anyone.

Memo from Marlene

Please remember that no matter what your body shape, you can look fantastic. The routine is, throw your head and shoulders back and put on your most important accessory: your smile! I can't stress it enough. Try it a few times in the mirror. You'll see that it really works.

89

YOUR CLOSET, YOUR SELF

N ORDER TO WEAR THE WONDERFUL wardrobe you've put together, you will need to find the clothes in your closet. Sorry, keeping your closet neat is essential to glamour. It's not very stylish to walk around in rumpled or stained clothing. And it's a waste of precious time looking for something to wear because your clothes are disorganized. These are all problems that can be quickly fixed with a neat and tidy closet. Don't worry; it's easy once you have the right tools and tricks. Here are a few ways to tackle that monster (aka that giant mound of clothing) in your bedroom.

By Clothing Type

THIS IS THE MOST PRACTICAL WAY TO OR-ganize closet. Sort all the clothes in your closet by making piles on your bed of different items such as skirts, shirts, jeans, and pants. Once you have everything sorted, figure out the best place in your closet for each type of clothing. Then hang all the skirts together, all your dresses together, and so on. Shirts

are folded on one shelf, sweaters on another, and pants on a third.

By Color

IF YOU THINK OF YOUR-self as artistic and like to experiment with color, this may be a more inspir-ational way for you to get dressed. Simply organize your wardrobe by color.

By Outfit

THIS IS FOR THE PERSON WHO DOESN'T want to waste a second getting dressed in the morning. Once you've crafted an A+ outfit, hang it all on one hanger (pants folded through a hanger with a shirt over it and shoes underneath). If not all the pieces fit, hang the items next to one another. You'll be ready in a flash. If you use this method, remember to mix up your outfits and try new ones from time to time to avoid a fashion rut.

Cheat Sheet!

IF YOU ARE A SHOE-AHOLIC, it can be hard to keep track of all the shoes piling up in the closet. Here's a tip from a stylist: Keep your shoes in their boxes, take photos of each pair, and paste them on the outside of the box. You'll never waste time searching for those snazzy sneaks again.

CARE PACKAGE

GETTING STAINS IS EXPECTED when you're having fun, but it doesn't have to ruin your favorite dress forever. Take care of your clothes and they'll take care of you. Making sure your clothes are clean and ready to go is as easy as one-two-three. Just follow the steps below. If you think you're naturally sloppy, don't worry. It takes only two weeks to break a bad habit, so a little discipline will keep your wardrobe in tip-top shape.

Step One: Treat Stains Quickly

STAINS ARE A PART OF LIFE. WHO HASN'T gotten chocolate cake on her dress at a birthday party? You should have fun in your clothes and not worry about them. The good news is that most stains can be removed if you act fast. If you toss that party dress on your closet floor and wait until laundry day to deal with the chocolate stain, you're sunk. No one is saying you should rush home from the party festivities to deal with your duds, but try to tackle the mini-accident within a couple of hours—the sooner the better. There are a lot of great stain-fighting products on the market, but sometimes good old soap and water

Memo from Marlene

Here's my favorite stain-fighting secret. It's so easy, you'll never believe it. But trust me, it works! Fruit-based stains, such as grape juice or tomato sauce, will instantly vanish if you pour boiling water over them.

94

will do the trick. Before you hit that stain with a spray, try using a dishwashing soap solution of one tablespoon of soap for every ten ounces of water. Rub the solution into the stain vigorously and blot with a towel or dishrag. Then rinse with cold water. You can try the same thing with club soda if you see that you didn't get it all.

Step Two: Wash Properly

IF YOU'VE EVER DONE A LOAD OF LAUNDRY and had everything come out pink, you know the importance of smart washing. Follow these rules.

Read the labels: Most garments have a sewn-in tag with specific instructions, but the symbols can be hard to decipher. Here's how the main ones translate.

SOME LABELS YOU WILL FIND

WASHING INSTRUCTIONS

machine wash, COLD   machine wash, WARM

machine wash, HOT

BLEACHING INSTRUCTIONS

 bleach   do not bleach

DRYING INSTRUCTIONS

 tumble dry, NO HEAT   ⊙ tumble dry, LOW HEAT

⊙⊙ tumble dry, MEDIUM HEAT   ⊙⊙⊙ tumble dry, HIGH HEAT

IRONING INSTRUCTIONS

 Iron with LOW HEAT   Iron with MEDIUM HEAT

Iron with HIGH HEAT

DRY CLEANING INSTRUCTIONS

◯ Dry clean   ⊗ Do not dry clean

Separate garments: White and dark colors should always be washed in separate loads to prevent running.

Go green: Here are a few ways you can save water when doing your laundry:

My Notes
Wash woolen sweaters inside out in cold water by hand or on the gentle cycle of the washing machine.

97

- Adjust the machine's water level when doing a small load.
- Hand wash several items at the same time.
- Wash only full loads.

Use the correct machine settings: The regular wash cycle is good for durable clothes, like jeans and sweats, or heavily soiled items. Permanent press is for everyday attire. The delicate cycle is for lightweight items, such as a nightgown. Use hot water for whites, warm water for regular loads, and cold water for bright colors. As for drying, refer back to the care labels and remember that too much heat can ruin some clothing. During warmer weather, give your clothing a summer-fresh smell (and go green!) by drying it on an outdoor clothesline.

Step Three: Store Safely

AFTER TAKING CARE TO KEEP YOUR CLOTHES clean, you'll want to store them properly so they will look clean and fresh.

Know when to fold: Only certain garments should be folded, while others should be hung up. For example, sweaters will pull out of shape if you try to hang them. Casual pants, such as jeans and khakis, can also be folded, and so can T-shirts.

Hang the rest: Most delicate clothing looks best when it's hung on a hanger. If at all possible, use wooden or plastic hangers. The special padded hangers are good for delicates, such as a silk party dress—and they look pretty too!

TAKING YOUR LOOK
ON THE ROAD

YOU HAVE A CLOSET FULL OF CLOTHES and know how to care for them too. Now here's your ultimate fashion challenge: Can you put together a great look on the go? Models are constantly traveling, so they need to pack smart and light and they have to appear fashionable and together wherever they are. That means every single item in their totes must be essential—and chic! Hold yourself to the same standard when you spend the night at a friend's house. It's easy with the ultimate sleepover prep guide below.

Make sure you have everything on the checklist on the following pages before you dash out for a slumber party or a Saturday night sleepover, and your overnight stay is sure to be a success.

☐ Overnight bag: Go for a lightweight but durable fabric

like canvas or nylon in a bold pattern. (Even your bag can express something about your style.) Make sure there are inside pockets to help you stay organized.

☐ Toiletry kit: Keep this stocked with a toothbrush and toothpaste, floss, face wash, moisturizer, and a hairbrush. That way it'll be ready to go when you are.

☐ Cute pj's: This is a total must. For an updated look, try a soft T-shirt with matching boy shorts. You'll look cute when caught raiding the fridge.

☐ Good book or magazine: Never leave home without one. You don't know when you might have trouble falling asleep.

☐ Address book with important telephone numbers: Get a nice, slim version to keep stashed away in your overnight bag—you never know what kind of emergency can come up.

☐ **Outfit for the next day:** Don't slink out of the house in yesterday's jeans. Start the day fresh in a whole new getup.

Memo from Marlene

When you are staying at a friend's overnight, it's important to be a good houseguest. I always recommend bringing a hostess gift, especially if you're going to someone's place for the first time. A small scented candle wrapped nicely or a bouquet of handpicked flowers work well. But you can also bring a craft item you've made in school, like a picture frame or bowl. A small item for the person who is hosting you is the perfect way to make a good impression (in most cases, it's someone's mom or dad). You'll get invited back again and again!

chapter 5

JUST ASK MARLENE

NOW THAT YOU HAVE LEARNED THE fundamentals of fashion, and a few fun extras, you're practically an expert. But that doesn't mean there isn't more to know. Whenever the models I work with have questions about style or design, they always say, "JAM!" or Just Ask Marlene! That's because I always have the answers. Here are a few of their questions I've decided to share with you. For more, visit JustAskMarlene.com.

jam
JUST ASK MARLENE®

I don't like to wear heels, because they kill my feet. What other kind of shoes can I wear that will look cute with fancy dresses?

—Chloe

SAY HELLO TO YOUR NEW BEST FRIEND, THE ballet flat! This timeless classic is the perfect shoe to wear with any pretty dress or skirt. Not only will you look elegant, but you'll also save your feet and avoid any back pain associated with heels. The great news is that ballet flats come in every color, pattern, and material under the sun. While they look wonderful for formal occasions, don't relegate them only to parties. Ballet flats look just as fabulous with jeans and even a nice pair of shorts. They'll have you dancing for joy.

I've been invited to a "trunk show" by my friend's mom, who is a designer. I was too embarrassed to ask, but what is a trunk show?

—Jenny

A TRUNK SHOW IS AN EVENT WHERE A designer or a sales representative shows up at a boutique or department store with a trunk (literally), filled with his or her merchandise. The people invited to these shows are always the store's best clients. So you are a pretty lucky girl to get a ticket to such an exclusive event! At a trunk show, a designer shows off styles from the upcoming season so that the A-list crowd can purchase items before they've even hit the stores. Even if you don't make any purchases at the trunk show your friend's mom invited you to, make sure you are appropriately dressed (no belly shirts or jeans, please). And enjoy the show!

> The most popular girl in my school wears short skirts, and now a lot of the other girls are copying her. I don't like short skirts. I don't like skirts at all. But should I wear one anyway?
> —Rochelle

IF YOU DON'T FEEL COMFORTABLE—WHETHER it's in a skirt, or hanging out with a particular crowd—you

107

need to listen to and respect your feelings. There's no law that says you have to wear a short skirt just because every-one else is doing it. But if you want to set your own style *and* be part of the crowd, you might want to give some thought to wearing a skort. Half shorts, half skirt, this hybrid looks like a skirt from the outside but are shorts on the inside. You will look cute and be able to sit down or walk up the steps at school worry free.

Fun Fact

Did you know that most people wear 20 percent of their clothing 80 percent of the time and 80 percent of their clothes 20 percent of the time?

Test your knowledge!

1. Why is white a good color to wear in summer?

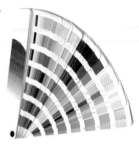

2. Which item does NOT belong in your overnight bag for a sleepover?

A. Toothbrush

B. Pajamas

C. Hostess gift

D. Whoopee cushion

E. Magazine or book

F. Change of clothes

3.

How do you get a fruit stain out of your favorite shirt?

4.

What is the job of a stylist on a photo shoot?

5.

What is the real way to be fashionable?

1. White reflects the sun, so it doesn't absorb heat and keeps you cool. But don't ignore white for winter, when it becomes a bold fashion choice. 2. D. Whoopee cushion—unless you're planning on pranking your friend. 3. Pour boiling water over the stain and watch it disappear like magic. 4. The stylist shops for the wardrobe or picks clothes and accessories from a designer's line and styles them on the model. Cool job, huh? 5. Have fun with your style. Let clothes be an extension of your incredible personality. Don't worry about rushing out to buy the latest trends. Finally, experiment with lots of looks—the true beauty comes from you.

epilogue

NOW THAT YOU'VE REACHED THE end of the book I hope you've learned how to help your inner beauty shine through and how to find a style that really works for the unique person you are. As you get older and your style becomes second nature, just remember to always be the special, beautiful person you are from the inside out.

Check out the
**Behind the
Scenes at the JAM
Photo Shoot**
video online!
JustAskMarlene.com

ACKNOWLEDGMENTS

T WAS A SUMMER LUNCH WITH BARBARA Marcus, my friend and agent, where we conceived of the books. If it weren't for Barbara and the need to eat, these books would not have been written. The team at Simon & Schuster led by my editor, Emily Lawrence, helped me create what I believe will be classic lifestyle guides for young teens for years to come. Gloria Norwich and Judy Gitenstein are the special people who always made certain my voice sang throughout. The photographer, Anna Palma, along with my models from Wilhelmina Kids & Teens, helped make the images in my head a beautiful reality. And then, of course, there's my sister, Maxine Bessin, who gave me perspective along the way, just as she always has. During this process, I have realized that the collection has become the most meaningful thing in my career, as I hope that the words on these pages will make the sometimes complex adolescent experience just a little more enjoyable.

JUST ASK MARLENE ®

Read these books by

Marlene Wallach

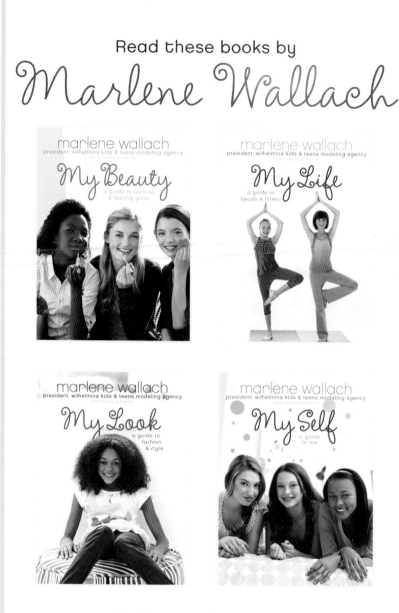

marlene wallach
president, wilhelmina kids & teens modeling agency

My Beauty
a guide to looking
& feeling great

marlene wallach
president, wilhelmina kids & teens modeling agency

My Life
a guide to
health & fitness

marlene wallach
president, wilhelmina kids & teens modeling agency

My Look
a guide to
fashion
& style

marlene wallach
president, wilhelmina kids & teens modeling agency

My Self
a guide
to me

Collect them all!

Amazing, crazy, wild and wonderful. Being a girl is all that and a lot more. Every day brings something new. Friends. Family. School. Sports. Hobbies. Clothes. Make-up... Boys!!! Jam wants to know what's happening with you.

Here at jam you become part of a huge community of girls from around the world who can't wait to share everything about their lives and learn about you. And where else will you be able to get the inside scoop and greatest and latest tips on

modeling • fashion • **beauty** • fitness • self-esteem • **fun**

This is an incredible time to be a girl. Never before have there been so many exciting activities, cool ideas, and magical possibilities.

Let's go for it! Come celebrate yourself at jam.

www.justaskmarlene.com